THE Living EARTH

What can we learn from observing the world around us?

Literature

Acorn 2
poem by Valerie Worth

Monarch Butterflies 4
nonfiction by Bianca Lavies

The Raccoon Brigade 22
fiction by Pat Kertzman

page 4

Related Readings and Projects

Meet the Press 3
research project

Wings of Flight 20
fine arts connection

Travel Light 21
social studies/mathematics connection

Born Free 29
writing connection

Designed for Defense 30
science connection

Reader Response 32
critical thinking

page 22

acorn

by Valerie Worth

An acorn
Fits perfectly
Into its shingled
Cup, with a stick
Attached
At the top,

Its polished
Nut curves
In the shape
Of a drop, drawn
Down to a thorn
At the tip,

And its heart
Holds folded
Thick white fat
From which
A marvelous
Tree grows up:

I think no better
Invention or
Mechanical trick
Could ever
Be bought
In a shop.

Meet the Press

Would you like to spend a day in the park? Who wouldn't! America boasts more than 83 million acres of national parks. And like the acorn in the poem you just read, each one is special too. Whatever type of living earth you want to explore, it's all in America's national parks. Below are some of America's favorites:

- **Acadia–Maine**
- **Badlands–South Dakota**
- **Carlsbad Caverns–New Mexico**
- **Crater Lake–Oregon**
- **Everglades–Florida**
- **Grand Canyon–Arizona**

- **Haleakala–Hawaii**
- **Hot Springs–Arkansas**
- **Olympic–Washington**
- **Petrified Forest–Arizona**
- **Shenandoah–Virginia**
- **Yellowstone–Wyoming**

Make a press kit for your favorite national park. Here's how:

Gather Information

1. Read about each of these parks in encyclopedias, travel books, or on websites. The official website for America's national parks is http://www.nps.gov/.
2. Jot down notes on the parks. Then pick the park that interests you most.
3. Get detailed facts about the park you choose. For example, what are some of the park's attractions? What species of wildlife make their home in the park? When did it become a national park?

Organize and Draw Conclusions

4. What are the most important aspects of the park you selected? List the key features.

Write and Present

5. A press kit includes a press release—an article about the park. It would also include some or all of the following items: fact sheets that describe plant life, wildlife, climate, elevation, and park history; brochures which explain the park's layout and guest features; a calendar of upcoming events; "photographs" (sketches or illustrations); and a videotape.
6. Arrange all the materials in a folder, and decorate the cover. Your press kit should encourage people to visit your chosen park.

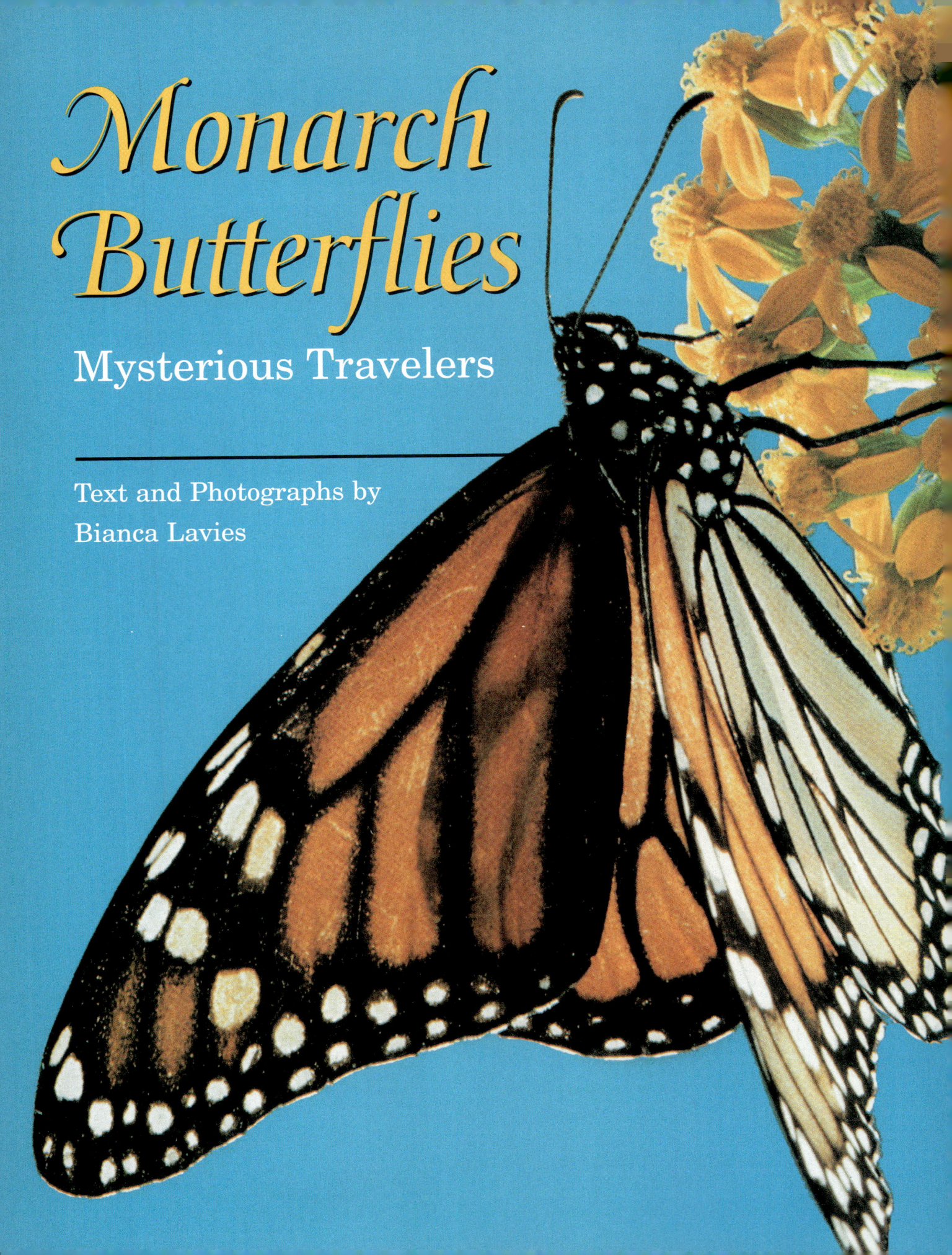

Monarch Butterflies
Mysterious Travelers

Text and Photographs by
Bianca Lavies

Look carefully at the brilliant orange-and-black wings of these adult monarch butterflies. How translucent they are against the light. And how seemingly frail. Tiny scales, which brush off in the hand like dust, give the wings their iridescent color.

How is it possible for such delicate insects to fly thousands of miles south in migration? Yet every autumn millions do, even embarking on a return trip north. Other butterflies migrate, but the monarch is the only butterfly that makes a round trip.

In summer monarchs are found over much of the continental United States and parts of southern Canada. But where do they go to avoid the killing frosts of winter? Is it to the same place every year? For decades one scientist sought answers to such questions. This is the story of how he solved part of the mystery of these enchanting, fragile travelers.

Ever since it hatched from a tiny egg two weeks ago, this caterpillar has done nothing but eat and rest and eat again. First, it devoured its egg case. Then, the caterpillar turned its strong jaws on the milkweed plant where its mother, a monarch butterfly, had laid her eggs. Milkweed leaves are the only food monarch caterpillars eat.

The caterpillar is one stage of the monarch life cycle from egg to adult butterfly. Another name for the caterpillar is *larva*.

This monarch larva grew so fast that every three or four days it had to shed its skin, or *molt*. A new layer of skin, bigger and brighter each time, was right there under the old one. After four molts the caterpillar is two inches long, full grown. Very soon it will stop eating and seek a shaded, sheltered spot to begin the next stage of its life.

To the underside of a twig the caterpillar attached a wad of silk, spun from a gland near its mouth. To this it fastened another little pad, or button, of silk. Then it grasped the silk

The Living Earth

button with its hind legs and hung upside down for between twelve and nineteen hours. Finally, stretching and pulsating, the caterpillar shed its skin for the last time.

The result of this final molt is the beautiful pale green chrysalis pictured here—something no longer a caterpillar but not yet a butterfly.

At first, the chrysalis is soft and damp. But as it dries in the air, it stiffens, turning the color of jade. Inside, cells begin to grow and multiply, replacing fleshy caterpillar features with the slender body and graceful wings of an adult butterfly. During this *metamorphosis,* or change of form, the insect (called a *pupa*) does not eat or drink.

Notice the sparkling gold spots. The word *chrysalis* comes from the Greek word *chrysos,* meaning "gold." Some scientists believe the spots control color in the developing wings.

During pupation, which takes from nine to fifteen days, depending on the temperature, the chrysalis changes from blue-green to dark gray. Just before the insect hatches, the outer shell becomes so clear that the orange-and-black pattern of the adult butterfly's wings shows through.

Somehow, newly formed monarchs can sense weather conditions from inside their chrysalises; they rarely emerge except on warm, sunny days. The clear chrysalis case cracks, and the adult butterfly pushes out. Hanging on to the case, it pumps blood from its body into hollow spaces between the two parallel membranes of each wing.

As the wings expand, the monarch opens and closes them in the drying sunlight and air. Two hours may pass before the wings are firm enough for flight. During this time the monarch clings tightly to its case. A fall could damage its wings or expose it to attacks from mice, shrews, or ants.

When the wings are stiff and strong, the butterfly is ready. In the warm sun, it takes off with a quiet swoosh to search for its first adult meal.

The adult monarch no longer has the caterpillar's chewing mouth parts, nor does it eat leaves. Instead, it has a hollow drinking tube called a *proboscis,* which it uses like a straw to suck nectar from deep inside flowers. When the butterfly first emerges from its chrysalis, it coils and uncoils the two halves of its proboscis to zip them into one long sucking tube. The proboscis tucks neatly away under the monarch's head when not in use.

Taste sensors on the butterfly's feet and smell receptors on the surface of the antennae help the monarch find and identify its food.

Monarchs that emerge in spring and early summer mate within about four days. Then the females busy themselves laying creamy yellow eggs on milkweed plants, sipping nectar from flowers, and drinking water from streams and puddles. A month or so later, both males and females die; in the meantime, a new generation of caterpillars is on its way to becoming butterflies.

Monarchs that emerge in late summer and autumn, however, lead longer, more far-reaching lives. The shorter, cooler days of early fall postpone the development of their reproductive organs. This, plus changes in light and temperature, perhaps along with other factors not yet understood, cues these monarchs to take to the skies, migrating hundreds or even thousands of miles across the continent to warmer wintering grounds.

They are strong, fast fliers, reaching speeds of ten to thirty miles per hour. Along the way, they sip from nourishing plants, fattening themselves for the coming winter. Monarchs are unable to fly when the temperature drops below fifty-five degrees Fahrenheit, so at night they roost on trees or bushes, then continue on during the warmer daytime.

People often wondered about the fluttering monarchs that filled the skies or clustered together on trees—usually the same trees year after year—from August to October. Researchers

The Living Earth

believed that monarchs west of the Rocky Mountains migrated to the coast of California. But where did the eastern monarchs go?

Since 1937, Dr. Fred Urquhart had been trying to discover where the eastern monarchs spent their winters. He and Norah, his wife and research assistant, tagged thousands of monarchs with labels that did not impede flight. Each tag carried a number and a request to mail it to the University of Toronto, where Dr. Urquhart worked.

Eventually children and adult volunteers all over North America helped with the tagging and also reported information about labeled monarchs they found. A picture began to emerge: Most monarchs that crossed the eastern United States seemed headed for Mexico.

Norah Urquhart wrote to newspapers in Mexico, asking people there to report sightings and help with tagging.

An American named Ken Brugger wrote back from Mexico City, offering to look for monarchs as he traveled the country with his dog, Kola, in his motor home. Shortly thereafter he married Cathy, a Mexican woman. She was a great help in the search because she could question local villagers in Spanish.

Ken, Cathy, and Kola—often with a guide—spent months following steep trails in the Sierra Madre Mountains. After about a year of searching, they were trekking up a two-mile-high peak in the early morning when they noticed a few monarchs circling downward. Local woodcutters had told them of swarms of butterflies nearby. Sure enough, a little higher, the ground proved littered with monarch wings—a sign that mice, birds, and other predators had been at work.

Near the summit, the trail of broken wings veered off into a dark forest of *oyamels,* local fir trees. At first glimpse, it seemed the trees were clothed in layers of dead brownish black leaves. But as sunlight pierced the dense evergreen forest, Cathy and Ken saw flashes of brilliant orange. They were looking at tens

of millions of monarch butterflies hanging from tree trunks and branches, and covering the ground like a thick carpet, wings closed in the cool morning air. The first monarch overwintering site in central Mexico had finally been found by researchers.

The Bruggers hurried to share the good news with the Urquharts in Canada. While waiting for them to arrange a trip down, Cathy and Ken worked every day, tagging butterflies in order to learn more about the northward migration to come. They also found more than half of the dozen or so overwintering sites that were eventually documented within a three-hundred-square-mile radius.

Some of the butterflies, like the one that has settled on Kola *(right)*, showed the wear and tear of their arduous journey. The spot on each hind wing—dark scales covering a scent pouch for attracting females—identifies this one as male.

At last the Urquharts arrived in Mexico City. Together with the Bruggers and photographer Bianca Lavies, they drove one hundred and fifty miles west into the mountains. Their rented bus wheezed and sputtered as it climbed seven thousand feet over rough, twisting roads to a small hotel surrounded by hundreds of white and red geraniums.

The next morning they drove farther up the mountain, winding through villages of simple homes gaily decorated with flowering plants. In one village they picked up their guide, Juan Sanchez *(left)*. After an hour and a half the road ended, and they drove on over a flat mountain plateau. Finally they parked the bus and continued on foot, Kola always by their side.

12   The Living Earth

For the next two hours they climbed a steep path, until, at ninety-eight hundred feet, they came upon a forest of tall oyamel trees. The Urquharts stared up in amazement, tears in their eyes. Here before them was the reality—astonishing and beautiful to behold—that had been the hope of a lifetime's research and hard work.

Everywhere they looked, butterflies blanketed the ground and hung from branches and tree trunks, their wings held closely together. Each time a ray of sunlight reached the butterflies, they fluttered into the sky, rising above the trees like puffs of orange-and-black smoke.

Monarchs have no internal heating system. They rely on the sun to warm them. In order not to overheat, they spread their four-inch wings and fly. By alternately basking to gain heat and flying to shed it, they regulate their body temperature. The oyamel forest high in the mountains was generally cool enough for them to remain dormant—a resting stage in which little nourishment is needed—but not so cold that they would freeze.

The monarchs hook their feet onto the needles and bark of the oyamels and rest securely, side by side. The thick forest growth offers shade on sunny days, keeps the temperature from falling too low at night, and provides shelter during storms.

Sometimes the clusters of monarchs get too heavy and an overloaded branch crashes to the ground. When Dr. Urquhart sat down to have his picture taken in the middle of just such a fallen pile of monarchs, with great good fortune his eye came to rest upon a butterfly bearing a white tag.

The tag enabled him to trace the butterfly back to Chaska, Minnesota, where, four months earlier, a teacher and his students had marked it. Traveling two thousand miles over mountains and rivers, congested cities and wide-open spaces,

this featherweight flier had journeyed to the very stand of oyamels where its great-grandparents had probably overwintered—and where its great-grandchildren would, in all likelihood, arrive next year.

While the Urquharts and Bruggers were busy tagging, crackling twigs more often than not announced the arrival of cows plodding through the brush. They trampled the thick carpet of butterflies, sucking them up by the dozens with large circular sweeps of their tongues. A local farmer told Cathy Brugger that his cows got fat during the winter from eating so many monarchs.

In the chill dawn air, when the butterflies were too cold to move, birds were also a menace. The birds picked them off the upper branches, stood on the monarchs' wings, and ate their fleshy abdomens. Butterflies with torn wings, broken antennae, and missing legs were common findings.

Spring comes early to the Sierra Madre Mountains, bringing with it the development of the females' reproductive organs and the cue to migrate once again. On warm, sunny days in January, the monarchs cluster at streams and marshy areas to drink water, a sign that they are ready to mate and head north. The females store sperm from the males, then fly off, laying fertilized eggs on milkweed plants along their route north. In about three days these eggs hatch; the adult butterflies that finally emerge also head north.

In May or early June, hardy migrant females reach the very same areas where they first nibbled milkweed leaves as caterpillars. Here they lay their last eggs, bringing to a close the eight to ten months of their migrant lives. But soon they are followed by their offspring, busily dotting the landscape with their own eggs. This generation and its offspring live only a month, however. By the end of August and early September, three or four generations are in the more northern breeding regions. Then shorter days and cooler temperatures cue the last generation. It is time to migrate. The cycle begins again.

Discovery of the Mexican overwintering grounds is considered the most important development in the study of monarch butterflies in the twentieth century. It was hoped the sites could be kept secluded, but thousands of tourists flocked to visit them. Now sanctuaries are being created by cooperating governments and wildlife groups. Logging also threatens the forest havens, however.

Elsewhere, other conditions endanger the monarchs. Herbicides are killing milkweed plants in monarchs' summer habitats and along their migration routes. Real-estate development encroaches on many of their roosting sites. Only time will tell whether or not we care enough to help the monarch butterfly ensure the survival of its species.

Bianca Lavies feels that being part of the expedition that led the Urquharts to the monarch overwintering sites in the Sierra Madre Mountains was a highlight of her eighteen-year career with National Geographic. "It was a great honor to witness the very emotional moment when the Urquharts saw the realization of their life's work for the first time," she says. "But it was not until fifteen days later that I felt that I had my best photographic day.

"After our usual midmorning snack of potatoes baked in the fire, we scrambled down a steep hill (eight minutes down, one hour up!) to a small mountain stream. It was a warm, sunny day, so the monarchs were very active. Many fluttered in the sky. Others crowded together in large colorful patches along the stream's muddy edges. They pushed each other, competing for more space and dipping their proboscises in the mud to quench their thirst. I worked frantically to keep up with the light, which moved rapidly across the water as the sun came and went behind the trees. I worked on low angles, squatting with my knees in the ice-cold water, ripping my pants on the rocks, slithering like a snake over the ground, covering my white T-shirt with mud. I kept seeing new angles and felt very excited.

"When I stepped back, I noticed magnificent reflections of monarchs crowding the edge of the water, their translucent wings backlit a bright orange as the sun shown through. I worked till I was sure I had captured this spectacular sight, then packed my cameras and climbed up to Cathy and Ken, who had been busy tagging.

"Cathy laughed when she saw the mud, the ripped pants, the dirty streaks of perspiration running down my face. 'You look like a little pig,' she said.

"But I didn't care. I would not have missed it for anything."

Wings of Flight

You can't reach all the way from your home to the monarch butterfly's winter home in the Sierra Madre Mountains, . . . or can you? You can bridge the distance by sending a symbolic butterfly to Mexico.

What You Do

1. On an 8 1/2" x 11" sheet of paper, draw a monarch butterfly. Use what you learned from *Monarch Butterflies* to make sure your drawn butterfly is factually correct, from its proboscis to its wings. Be sure your butterfly is the correct size too.
2. Cut out the butterfly and mount it on stiff board.
3. Tag the butterfly with your name, school, and address.
4. Add a brief message to a child in Mexico who might care for your butterfly during the winter months. You can write the message in English or Spanish.
5. Use string to suspend your butterfly from the classroom ceiling. Help your classmates suspend their butterflies to make a flock.

Use What You Learn

6. How could you actually send your butterflies? Brainstorm ways to locate a sixth-grade student in Mexico who might keep your butterfly over the winter. If possible, send your butterfly to your partner in Mexico. Have your partner send his or her butterfly to you in the spring.

Travel Light

Where do the monarch butterflies go each autumn? For many years it was a mystery, but now we know that monarchs from the eastern part of the United States travel to the Sierra Madre Mountains in Mexico. Wouldn't it be nice to take a long trip every fall? You probably can't take a real trip to Mexico, but you can take a virtual one!

Look at a map of the United States and Mexico. Choose a city east of the Rocky Mountains and retrace the route the monarch butterflies follow as they migrate from this city to Mexico. But since you're a person, you have to travel on roads, rather than fly through the air!

What You Do

1. First, map the *shortest* round-trip car route. You'll probably travel on interstate highways.

2. Then, map the *most scenic* round-trip car route. This is the route that has the best views. You might drive on local roads and pass through mountains, by lakes, and near the ocean. Since your trip will take place in the fall, you may want to travel through forests so you can see the leaves turning colors on the trees.

3. As you map out your routes, do the following:
- Write out the directions for each route.
- Compute the mileage each direction as well as round trip for both routes.
- Decide which route is the best and why you think so. Justify your choice in a persuasive paragraph.

Use What You Learn

4. Monarch butterflies face many dangers when they migrate. Humans taking car trips do too. What can you do to make car trips safer?

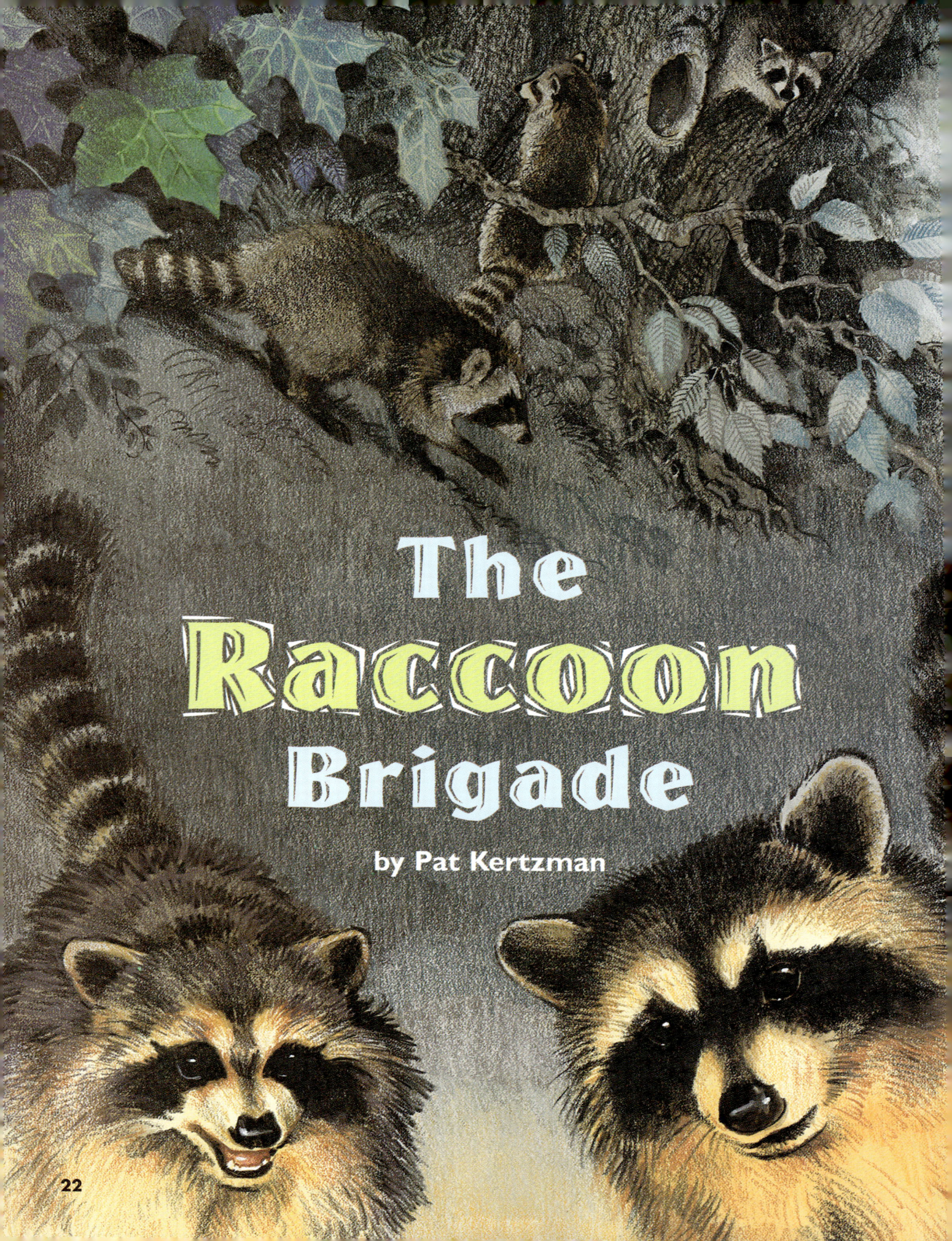

The Raccoon Brigade

by Pat Kertzman

For a long time we lived in peace with the raccoons. Their home was a clump of hollow trees across the street. They were like intriguing cousins from another country, our non-English-speaking relatives.

Sometimes Mom let me leave a bowl of leftovers behind the garage for them. They gobbled vegetables, casseroles, fish, cereal, nuts, fruit, sweets—just about anything. I made sure we supplied all the major food groups. The neighbors complained of raccoons raiding their garbage cans in the middle of the night, but they never touched ours. We had an understanding.

My sister, Carla, took a picture of the giant raccoon we called Hugo shucking an ear of corn. He clamped the ear between his hind feet and removed every leaf and strand with his nimble little hands. Hugo was concentrating so hard that he hardly blinked when the camera flashed. Carla captioned the snapshot, "Butter would be perfect."

Carla and I named each new kit and kept a record of births and deaths. We got their personalities down on paper too. You might think raccoons are all pretty much the same. It isn't true. Adrienne had a large, pointy mask and a scraggly tail. Maxwell limped and had a bald gouge in his side. Hugo was gigantic and fearless—always first at the dinner bowl and last to leave. He'd growl and skirmish over a piece of scrambled egg. Molly was happy and flirtatious. She chirped and trilled and purred whenever we looked at her. Her mother sometimes dragged her away by the scruff, scolding all the way.

Our dogs, Garrison the boxer and Murphy the Dalmatian, were young and spunky. The raccoons' midnight escapades sent Murphy into furious growling and howling. "Don't you care what's happening here?" she'd bark accusingly. "We're losing control!"

On summer nights when it was too hot to sleep, the whole family would go out with a lantern to look at the raccoons. Samuel would quietly ponder the moon, the trees full of eyes, and the lantern-cast shadows. Then two things happened that changed everything.

The Living Earth

In the Year of the Raccoons, Carla was thirteen, I was eleven, and our brother, Samuel, was two. Samuel was growing and needed a room of his own, so a man helped Dad turn our attic into a living area. All that was left above it was a crawlspace. Around the same time, the village council decided that Grange Avenue was too busy and congested and should be expanded. The old trees were chopped down before we could protest. Forever there, gone in a day. Where would the raccoon families go? Not too far, we hoped.

Carla started hearing noises at night above her room. She had an active imagination, so my parents assured her, "Go to sleep; it's nothing." Eventually everyone heard something, but we were too busy to investigate the noise.

One wet Saturday in April, Mom and Dad noticed a hole in the back of the house leading to the crawlspace. They raced into the house and headed straight for the stairway. They crawled through the grungy space like crocodiles on a mission and found a litter of four kits bawling for supper. Mother Raccoon was nowhere to be seen.

My parents emerged from the crawlspace dirty and damp and wondering what to do. "Let's call the DNR," Dad suggested. The people at the Department of Natural Resources said to remove the kits and place them in a shallow container in the yard. Adult raccoons would probably retrieve them. Then we should board up the hole. The raccoons would get the message and stay away. I was proud that the raccoons had used our house for a nursery and sorry that they couldn't stay.

"They're wild, and they always will be," Dad said when I argued.

"Neighbors are one thing; live-ins are another," Mom added.

Mom and Dad boarded up the hole tightly with lumber and metal fencing. We cleaned a shallow tub from the garage and lined it with an old yellow blanket. We placed the kits inside and left them oatmeal with milk and cooked apples. We covered them up and hoped for the best. Nobody said anything, but I'm sure we all feared that a hawk, fox, or neighborhood hound would find them first.

The Living Earth

I kept Murphy and Garrison away from the babies. I could tell Murphy thought we were cracked for keeping baby raccoons in a tub in the backyard. "Your opinion doesn't count," I informed her. She cocked her head in complete disagreement.

"We're doing the right thing," Mom told the wall as we picked at our supper in silence. Even Samuel was quiet.

"We're doing the right thing," I repeated to Murphy.

The next day the kits were gone. The yellow blanket looked lonely in the tub, speckled by the morning sun. Raccoon prints were everywhere.

Late that night an incredible racket woke me up. I flew out of bed, grabbed my robe, and met Carla in the hall. Mom and Dad were already up. Dad turned the floodlights on, and we all ran to the backyard. Neighbors were gathering. Mouths moved, and brows wrinkled in alarm, but we couldn't hear a word. The screeches were deafening.

One by one, eleven adult raccoons scaled the back of our house. The journey was treacherous, but they were expert climbers. They marched with purpose and spoke in raging tongues. The raccoons took turns working at the patched hole for over an hour—clawing, scratching, biting, instructing, and criticizing each other. Their efforts were impressive, but they only managed to ruin some of our siding. Finally they climbed down in orderly single file, as if they'd rehearsed, and walked away. They kept their backs to us. We were newly despicable, undeserving of a glance. Only one turned around for a final hiss. Then they were gone.

The neighbors stood around wondering at the spectacle. Why so many raccoons? Carla and I agreed that most of them were new to us. We had recognized only three. They must have recruited friends and cousins, aunts and uncles, even grandraccoons. It was a complete raccoon brigade. But why the protest?

We thought we might know.

The next morning Dad and I crept into the crawlspace and listened. Sure enough, a kit was huddled in the corner, mewing pitifully. We'd overlooked it, but the raccoons hadn't.

"You are one missed little kit," Dad told it.

It was damp and frosty that night. We covered the kit with blankets, and I worried like a new mother. Would it suffocate or freeze? Would that mongrel down the street who roamed at night find it first? How persistent are raccoons? I wondered. Would the search party return, or would they consider their duty done and hope gone?

Sometime that night, the woebegone kit was claimed from the tub. They were quiet this time, but footprints showed the raccoon brigade had returned.

We never saw our raccoon friends again, but I think of them often. I'm writing this so Samuel can remember too. The fact that we had their trust and then so completely betrayed them, knowingly or not, still makes me a little sad. I wonder if new kids are keeping track of births and deaths and food groups. Even if no one is, it's all right. The raccoons will be O.K. They have each other.

Born Free

Mom and Dad in "The Raccoon Brigade" realize that raccoons are wild and always will be. They tell their children that no matter how cute the raccoons are, the animals belong in the wild. Dogs, cats, and fish make great pets. So do gerbils and guinea pigs. Raccoons don't. Here are some reasons why:

- Raccoons are wild animals and cannot be tamed.
- Raccoons cannot be raised singly; they must interact with other raccoons to learn social skills and play.
- Raccoons pose very serious health problems for humans, such as rabies and *Baylisascaris procyonis* (the raccoon roundworm). Both diseases can be fatal to raccoons and humans.

Speak Out for Wild Animals

Write an editorial to the school newspaper to persuade readers that raccoons and other wild animals do not make good pets. Editorials are a kind of persuasive writing that uses reasons, facts, quotations from experts, details, statistics (numbers), and emotion to convince readers. First, read several newspaper editorials to use as models. Then, find additional facts about raccoons from "The Raccoon Brigade," in science books, or on the Internet. Be sure to revise, edit, and proofread your writing. Here's how your editorial should be organized:

Introduction
- the topic sentence
- the issue I'm exploring
- my opinion about the issue
- body paragraph
- evidence: facts, details, reasons, expert opinions

Conclusion
- summarize my points
- offer a recommendation

Designed for Defense

Nature is a tough place. It's often an "eat-or-be-eaten" existence for animals in the wild. Any physical encounter is a risk. Even if an animal wins a battle, it might be wounded. Then, the weakened animal could be attacked by predators and end up even more badly hurt. That's why many animals have defense strategies or natural camouflage that ward off attackers without the risk of bodily harm.

Below are five different species and the adaptations they have developed to help them survive. On a separate sheet of paper, explain the advantages and disadvantages of each adaptation. Then decide which of the adaptations you think are the most effective and why.

Armored Armadillos

With its bony *scutes* (plates) of armor covered by horn, the armadillo looks like a mammalian tank. Some armadillo species roll up into a ball to protect their bodies. Other armadillo species dig into the ground to protect their softer, vulnerable underparts.

Possum Play

Opossums pretend to be dead when seized by attackers. How the trick works isn't clear. Perhaps predators who don't feed on dead animals lose interest. We use the phrase "playing possum" to describe someone who pretends to be asleep or dead.

Prickly Porcupines

Porcupines have sharp quills that come off easily. When in danger, a porcupine will run backwards into its attacker and leave quills sticking into its skin. The crested porcupine's tail has rattle quills. Rather than get into a fight, this animal rattles its tail to frighten the attacker away.

Clash of the Antlers

Red deer have an impressive rack (set) of antlers. These antlers show strength and dominance that scare opponents.

Who Was That Masked Bandit?

Raccoons have stripes that help them blend into the woods where they live. And their faces have masks!

Call of the Wild

What You Need

- paper bags • paper plates • colored construction paper
- scissors • string • glue • tape

What You Do

How well do you blend into nature? Make a mask that would serve to camouflage you in your natural environment. Here's how:

1. Think about the setting in which you live. What kind of mask would help you blend into that setting? If you live near tropical gardens, you might cover your mask with bright flowers. If you live near a forest, your mask might be leafy and green. List at least five ideas.

2. Gather the materials you need for your mask. You can use a paper plate or a paper bag as the base.

3. Assemble your mask by adding the camouflage.

4. Test the mask by having a friend take a picture of you outdoors. Do you blend in with the rest of nature?

Use What You Learn

5. What other adaptations would protect you from harm in nature? Design an outfit that would help you blend in with your environment. Draw and label it. Write a description.

Reader Response

1. **Think About the Theme**

    What can we learn from observing the world around us? How can each of us help preserve our world? Think about Dr. Urquhart in *Monarch Butterflies* and the family in "The Raccoon Brigade." Consider the people you know and your efforts to help the living Earth. List some ways that you and your friends can help preserve our world.

2. **Ask a Question**

    If you were tracking the monarch butterflies with Bianca Lavies, what questions could you ask Dr. Urquhart to find out more about these fascinating creatures? Write at least three questions.

3. **Use New Vocabulary**

    What new and useful words did you learn? List them and then use at least eight in a crossword puzzle.

4. **Make Connections**

    What does each of these three literature selections reveal about the cycle of life? How are life cycles the same? How are they different?

5. **Analyze**

    What do you think were the most difficult aspects of tracking the monarch butterflies and dealing with the raccoons? Why?

32 The Living Earth